WE ARE A RAINBOW

Written and illustrated by
Nancy María Grande Tabor

 Charlesbridge

For Lynn and everyone who reaches out to bridge cultures

Bilingual books by Nancy María Grande Tabor:

ALBERTINA ANDA ARRIBA: EL ABECEDARIO
Albertina Goes Up: An Alphabet Book

CINCUENTA EN LA CEBRA: CONTANDO CON LOS ANIMALES
Fifty on the Zebra: Counting with the Animals

SOMOS UN ARCO IRIS
We Are a Rainbow

EL GUSTO DEL MERCADO MEXICANO
A Taste of the Mexican Market

Published by Charlesbridge Publishing, 85 Main Street,
Watertown, MA 02472 • (617) 926-0329 • www.charlesbridge.com

Library of Congress Cataloging-in-Publication Data is available upon request.

Printed in the United States of America
(hc) 10 9 8 7 6 5 4 3 2
(sc) 10 9 8 7 6 5 4 3

ISBN 0-88106-646-X (reinforced for library use)
ISBN 0-88106-417-3 (softcover)

This book was printed on recycled paper.

We are moving to a new country.

New places. New faces.

So many new and different things!

Where I come from, there
is a rabbit in the moon.

Here there is a man in the moon.

There the ocean is nice and warm.

Here the ocean is nice and cool.

There the leaves of the palm tree swayed next to my pink adobe house.

Here the oak branches wave next to my blue wooden house.

There we give handshakes, hugs,
and kisses to everyone.

Here handshakes are for new people and hugs and kisses for very special ones.

There I would eat tortillas for breakfast.

Here people have them for dinner.

To you, I may seem different.

But to me, you seem different, too.

I try hard to understand what you say.

You try to understand me, too.

When we do not
understand each other, we feel bad.
We fight. We hurt.

We cry. We separate.
We stop trying to find a way
to be together.

Apart. Alone. Please
stop and think.

Are we as different as we think?

I say *sol*. You say *sun*.

But no matter how we say it,
it is the same one.

We all like to run and play.

We all like to dance and sing.

We really are so much the same.

And it is much more fun to be together –
to share, to care, to smile, and to laugh.

Our tears and our smiles are like the rain and the sun.

They help our friendships to grow.

And friendships are like rainbows . . .
they shine for everyone!